AUTHENTICALLY
ANCHORED

Shonda Ramsey

Companion
WORKBOOK

Authentically
CREATED

For all who feel unrecognizable.

Have hope, for one day you'll soon discover your identity in a world filled with disappointment and find joy in a life you've never imagined through God's grace. I pray that throughout these pages you'll learn how to anchor yourself in Christ so you never find yourself at the bottom of the ocean again.

Disclaimer

This book was written with the Christian faith in mind, referencing verses from the Holy Bible and making mention of God, Father, Jesus, Lord, and Holy Spirit. I recognize there are many different religious beliefs; if your faith is different from Christianity, I encourage you to read my book with an open mind and apply your faith where applicable. It is important to note that I am an imperfect Christian, but I am always seeking to learn, to do, and to be better. The contents of this book are straight from my heart. It is my hope that you'll find comfort in the scriptures and companionship in the pages that lie before you.

Contents

Dedication

Disclaimer

Introduction 9

Chapter One: Grace in Deep Waters 15

Chapter Two: Who Am I? 25

Chapter Three: Never Truly Alone 35

Chapter Four: Seeing the Beauty in God's Design.............43

Chapter Five: Rebuilding Friendship 51

Chapter Six: Rediscover Your Passions 59

Chapter Seven: Forced to Pivot 69

Chapter Eight: Autopilot 77

Chapter Nine: Life Has a Meaning 85

Chapter Ten: Change is Hard 93

Chapter Eleven: Paint Chips = Progress..........................101

Chapter Twelve: It's Going to Be Okay 111

Chapter Thirteen: Love Yourself as God Loves You...........121

Chapter Fourteen: (Re)Build Your Community 129

Chapter Fifteen: Rediscovery of Joy...............................137

Chapter Sixteen: You Are Authentically Created 145

A Letter From Shonda

Introduction

To not only emerge from the bottom of the ocean but remain steadfast on the shore—authentically anchored in Christ—I knew I had to take action. This *Authentically Anchored Companion Workbook* breaks down the Anchor Points more in-depth than the book by offering you a chance to take even more actionable steps on your path to becoming authentically anchored in Christ.

What you can expect for each chapter:

A.N.C.H.O.R.E.D.—Affirm, Notate, Craft, Honor, Observe, Rebuild, Emerge, Dedicate

A–Affirm—Scripture Memorization: Rooting yourself in God's word is the necessary foundation for rediscovering your identity. (Philippians 4:13, *"I can do all this through him who gives me strength."*)

N–Notate—Scripture Application: Studying and applying God's word will help guide you on your path of rediscovery. (Psalm 119:105, *"Your word is a lamp for my feet, a light on my path."*)

C–Craft—Creative Exercise: Freedom of expression by allowing God to let your creativity flow. (Isaiah 64:8, *"Yet you, Lord, are our Father. We are the clay, you are the potter; we are all the work of your hand."*)

H–Honor—Prayer: Inviting Jesus to have a personal encounter with you. (Psalm 107:1–3, *"Give thanks to the Lord, for he is good; his love endures forever. Let the redeemed of the Lord tell their story—those he redeemed from the hand of the foe, those he gathered from the lands, from east and west, from north and south."*)

O–Observe—Exercise and Journal Prompt: A chance to see who you are at your core. (Matthew 22:37, *"Jesus replied: 'Love the Lord your God with all your heart and with all your soul and with all your mind.'"*)

R–Rebuild—Journal Prompt: A look into all you've endured and plans to rebuild your life going forward. (1 Peter 5:10, *"And the God of all grace, who called you to his eternal glory in Christ, after you have suffered a little while, will himself restore you and make you strong, firm and steadfast."*)

E–Emerge—Action Taking Exercise: The gentle nudge you may need to help you get up and get moving. These exercises are what will help break the pattern of being on autopilot. (Hebrews 13:5, *"Keep your lives free from the love of money and be content with what you have, because God has said, 'Never will I leave you; never will I forsake you.'"* Isaiah 9:2, *"The people walking in darkness have seen a great light; on those living in the land of deep darkness a light has dawned."*)

D–Dedicate—Journal Prompts & Dedication: Your promise to God that you are all in on being authentically anchored in Him. (Colossians 3:23–24, *"Whatever you do, work at it with all your heart, as working for the Lord, not for human masters, since you know that you will receive an inheritance from the Lord as a reward. It is the Lord Christ you are serving."*)

Resources to Have on Hand

This workbook is an interactive book, with encouragement to act on rediscovering your identity. There are resources listed here that I personally use daily and will help you maximize your experience. I recommend you gather as many of these items as possible and put them in a tote bag or some other small mobile container so you can take them with you wherever you choose to do the activities. I call this my *Growth Bag*.

Growth Bag Contents:
- Authentically Anchored Book and Companion Workbook
- Pocket or Digital Bible
  - YouVersion App (or other similar)
- Journal
- Pens
- Paper (loose)
- Colored pencils, markers, or crayons
- Mirror
- Sticky notes or a dry erase marker
- Spotify Playlist

A Curated Spotify Playlist that coordinates with *Authentically Anchored*

All that stands between you and rediscovering your identity is an open heart and mind. I ask that you give yourself grace and patience as you work through some difficult exercises to get to the root of who you are and rebuild your relationship with God.

Friend, I know you are hurting. You may be scared and alone in the darkness, longing for a hand to reach out and pull you to the surface. I know because I'm here beside you at the bottom of the ocean. You aren't alone; God wants you to know that He loves you and cares for you. Despite your broken moments, there is the possibility of finding joy in the life you've never imagined through God's grace and your resilience.

I hope that by sharing with you the action I took to find my footing again, you will come to know and understand more about who you are as you deepen your relationship with God. Will you join me as we swim to shore where I will weep with you, pray with you, and I will encourage you along the way?

Dedication

I, _____ , commit to not only reading Authentically Anchored but also promise to open my heart as I engage with, actively participate, and apply the Anchor Points provided for each chapter in this companion workbook as I begin to rebrand my life.

Signed,

Date: _____

My Prayer for You

I know it's a lot to ask you to commit to doing the hard work of rebuilding your life. You have been struggling for far too long, consider this companion workbook a lifeline, sent to you to help bring you to shore. I cannot promise that these exercises and activities will be earth shattering, but what I can promise is that they are thoughtfully created with the sole purpose of deepening your relationship with God as you learn to love the life you are living despite it not looking as you had envisioned.

The amount of time and effort you put into completing this companion workbook is entirely up to you and should be at a pace you are most comfortable with. What you'll get out of it is dependent upon the level of commitment to yourself and your relationship with God. There is no grade, there is no benchmark, there is only a stronger encounter with Jesus awaiting you.

Lord, I lift my friend up now. She has courageously agreed to take action by creating more space for you in her life. Please make your presence known as she does the hard work and faces herself in the mirror. Let her know how beautiful she is in your eyes. I pray, Lord, that upon completion of this workbook, she will have a renewed sense of hope and a heart filled with joy. Lord, thank you for bringing this beautiful woman to this place, at this exact moment in time. Amen.

I'm rooting for you as you take this next big leap of faith.
With Grace,
Shonda Ramsey

chapter one
Grace in Deep Waters

One of the hardest things to do after losing your identity is to face yourself in the mirror. I know how challenging it can be firsthand, which is why I consider it is the most important first actionable step for you to take. This is an action you should not force; you should take as much time as you need working up to it. There is no time deadline or expectation to do it right away. Facing yourself in the mirror is a reminder you that you are authentically created by God to be you. Allow Him to help you as you face your fears.

Affirm

Scripture Memorization: Write the following scripture and post it somewhere you'll see it every day. Maybe it's a bathroom mirror, refrigerator, or your home office. Memorize it and refer to it when you feel alone at the bottom of the ocean.

"When you pass through the waters, I will be with you; and when you pass through the rivers, they will not sweep over you. When you walk through the fire, you will not be burned; the flames will not set you ablaze." —Isaiah 43:2

Notate

Scripture Application: Reading the verse in Isaiah 43:2, how can this verse be applied to your life today?

_____

_____

_____

_____

_____

_____

_____

_____

_____

Craft

Creative Exercise: Assemble your *Growth Bag* with items you can use as you take action to rediscover your identity. Instructions for your *Growth Bag* were mentioned in the Introduction of this workbook. If you haven't had a chance to read the introduction yet, now is a good time to pause and read it. Once you're up to speed, come back to this section ready to engage with the activities below.

Items I added to my *Growth Bag*:

- ☐ _____
- ☐ _____
- ☐ _____
- ☐ _____
- ☐ _____
- ☐ _____
- ☐ _____
- ☐ _____
- ☐ _____
- ☐ _____
- ☐ _____
- ☐ _____

Honor

Prayer: *Heavenly Father, in this moment—whether I find myself sitting at the bottom of the ocean or standing on the shore—let me feel your presence now. Father, help me know that I am never alone in my struggles, that I am cherished, worthy, and enough. Please make your grace known to me in this season of my life. Give me strength to face each new day as I work on rebuilding my identity in you. Lord, thank you for extending your hand and helping me become anchored in you, Amen.*

Observe

- **Mirror Exercise:** Look at your reflection for no less than three minutes and acknowledge every physical feature you see.
- **Journal:** Reflect on your mirror exercise and answer the following question.

Write down everything you saw staring back at you and how you feel. (Good or bad, honesty is key.) Feel free to add doodles if you feel led to do so.

_____

_____

_____

_____

_____

_____

_____

_____

_____

_____

_____

_____

_____

_____

_____

_____

_____

_____

Doodles

Rebuild

How do I feel about everything that is going on in my life?

_____

_____

_____

_____

_____

_____

_____

_____

_____

_____

_____

How do I feel about where I am now? Spiritually, physically, and emotionally.

_____

_____

_____

_____

_____

_____

_____

_____

_____

_____

_____

_____

What do I hope to accomplish throughout the pages of this book?

_____
_____
_____
_____
_____
_____
_____
_____
_____
_____
_____
_____
_____
_____

Where do I hope to be by the end of this book?

_____
_____
_____
_____
_____
_____
_____
_____
_____
_____
_____
_____
_____
_____

Emerge

Action Taking Exercise: Spend time outside, near water, if possible, to sit silently in prayer. Ask God to meet you in the depths, and make His presence known. Use this space to jot down anything that comes to your mind while you complete this exercise.

_____

_____

_____

_____

_____

_____

_____

_____

_____

_____

_____

_____

_____

_____

_____

_____

_____

_____

_____

_____

_____

_____

_____

_____

_____

Dedicate

The areas in my life I want revived are:

_____

_____

_____

_____

_____

_____

This is important to me because:

_____

_____

_____

_____

_____

_____

_____

Declaration Statements

"I am" statement: Write a statement about who you feel you are in this very moment. *Example: I am hopeful.*

I am

_____

_____

"I hope to be" statement: Write a statement about who you hope to be by the end of this book. *Example: I hope to be confident in my identity.*

I hope to be

_____

_____

Chapter Two
Who Am I?

Allowing others to assign labels to our lives adds unnecessary weights to our anchor chain that threaten to keep us captive at the bottom of the ocean. I learned that to free myself from the pressure of all that weight, I had to shed those labels and the ones I put on myself. I want to encourage you to consider the weights you've added to your anchor chain. Are there any that you can remove today? By stripping it back to the basics, you will be able to start fresh, with a clean slate as you find yourself standing back on solid ground.

Affirm

Scripture Memorization: Write the following scripture and post it somewhere you'll see it every day. Maybe it's a bathroom mirror, refrigerator, or your home office. Memorize it and refer to it when you feel alone at the bottom of the ocean.

"See what great love the Father has lavished on us, that we should be called children of God! And that is what we are! The reason the world does not know us is that it did not know him." —1 John 3:1

Notate

Scripture Application: Reading the verse in 1 John 3:1, how can this verse be applied to your life today?

_____

_____

_____

_____

_____

_____

_____

_____

_____

Craft

Creative Exercise: You don't need to be an exceptional artist; stick figures are not only welcomed, they are highly encouraged! This exercise can be as simple or as elaborate as you want.

Doodle Exercise 1: Doodle yourself at the bottom of the ocean and what your surroundings look like. Draw your anchor and chain with labels. Write the terms others have labeled you on each link. (Example: unqualified) Write descriptive words in the spaces around you that describe how you feel in the depths as you are weighed down by these labels.

Doodle Exercise 2: Doodle yourself standing on solid ground holding one hand of Jesus, and draw His other hand holding your anchor. Write descriptive words around you that describe how you feel being pulled to safety and authentically anchored in Christ.

Honor

Prayer: *Heavenly Father, so many labels have been put on my shoulders that I no longer want to continue carrying. I pray that you give me strength and courage to remove every single label that doesn't serve me anymore. Help me to only pick up the one that matters most in this moment. I am your child, God. I pray that as the labels fall off, you help me reach the shore and find my footing on solid ground once more. I pray that you continue to work in me as I complete this book, opening myself up to allow more space for you in my life. Thank you, Lord, for carrying my anchor, Amen.*

Observe

- **Mirror Exercise:** Look in the mirror, lock eyes with yourself, and calmly ask "Who am I?" at the reflection staring at you. Take note of any movements in your reflection as you do this exercise.
- **{Optional} Mirror Exercises:** Shout, if you need to, "WHO AM I?!" at the reflection staring at you. Take note of any movements in your reflection as you do this exercise.
- **Journal:** The mirror exercise(s) made me feel... (Did it scare you, energize you, wake you up? Write about it.)

_____

_____

_____

_____

_____

_____

_____

_____

_____

_____

_____

Rebuild

Exercise: What labels have I picked up and placed on myself? Write down every single one on a sheet of paper, pray over it, rip it up, and toss it.

Write about what you experienced during the exercise, what you let go of, and how it made you feel.

_____

_____

_____

_____

_____

_____

_____

_____

_____

_____

In what ways can I reach up to God and allow Him to pull me up from deep waters?

_____

_____

_____

_____

_____

_____

_____

_____

_____

_____

Am I holding on too tightly? What control do I have to let go of to be pulled to safety?

_____

_____

_____

_____

_____

_____

_____

_____

_____

_____

_____

_____

Emerge

Action Taking Exercise: Spend time outside in the same spot as before, near water, if possible, to sit silently in prayer. Ask God to help you to shore and thank Him in advance for the work He is doing in you. Use this space to jot down anything that comes to your mind while you complete this exercise.

_____

_____

_____

_____

_____

_____

_____

_____

_____

_____

_____

_____

Dedicate

(Re)commit to God the promise of self-discovery in Him by writing a letter to Him.

_____

_____

_____

_____

_____

_____

_____

_____

_____

_____

_____

_____

_____

_____

_____

_____

Declaration Statements

"I am" statement: Write a statement about who you feel you are in this very moment. *Example: I am free to be me.*

I am

_____

_____

"I hope to be" statement: Write a statement about who you hope to be by the end of this book. *Example: I hope to be able to shed the weight of the labels.*

I hope to be

_____

_____

Chapter Three
Never Truly Alone

As you enter a season of solitude, I want to acknowledge how brave you are for giving it a chance to change your life. Whether you commit to one hour a week or more, the choice is yours to do. Solitude is the very best thing I have ever done for myself. In my time spent alone with God, I was able to remove all distractions and pour my heart out to God in a way that I hadn't ever done before. At times it was difficult, but nevertheless, I persisted and leaned into God more so that I could uncover who I was in Him. As you begin spending more time with God in prayer, may you remember that you are never truly alone.

Affirm

Scripture Memorization: Write the following scripture and post it somewhere you'll see it every day. Maybe it's a bathroom mirror, refrigerator, or your home office. Memorize it and refer to it when you feel alone at the bottom of the ocean.

"He says, 'Be still, and know that I am God; I will be exalted among the nations, I will be exalted in the earth.'" —Psalm 46:10

Notate

Scripture Application: Reading the verse in Psalm 46:10, how can this verse be applied to your life today?

_____

_____

_____

_____

_____

_____

_____

_____

_____

Craft

Creative Exercise: On a sheet of paper, write a letter of forgiveness to someone you have been unable to fully forgive. Once you have written your letter, destroy it (burn, rip, shred, etc.). Verbally say, "I forgive you, I bless you, I release you." Use this space to jot down anything that comes to your mind while you complete this exercise.

_____

_____

_____

_____

_____

_____

_____

_____

_____

_____

_____

_____

_____

_____

_____

Honor

Prayer: *Heavenly Father, I lift up my friend who is currently reading my book. Lord, her heart is weary, she feels alone and rejected by forces beyond her control. She isn't sure what the right next steps are and she has lost her sense of identity as a result of putting her hope in others. Lord, I pray that you help her put her hope back in you. That you open her heart to love and be loved again. I pray, Lord, that you remind her that she is authentically created to be the most beautiful person ever—herself. Lord, I lift her up to you, Amen.*

Observe

- **Exercise:** On a sheet of paper, write a letter of forgiveness to yourself, listing all the things you are letting go of that are holding you back. Once you have written your letter, fold it and tuck it away in your journal or bible. You will cross paths with it when you need it most.
- **Journal:** List 3 new habits you hope to introduce or re-introduce into your life to aid you in your faith.

Habit 1

Habit 2

Habit 3

Rebuild

Exercise: Enter a time of prayerful solitude. You select the duration you need to invite God in to help you complete these journal prompts.

The thought of a season of solitude makes me feel…

_____

_____

_____

_____

_____

_____

_____

What is one area of improvement for how I am showing up in my relationship with God?

_____

_____

_____

_____

_____

What is one area of improvement for how I am showing up in my friendships?

_____

_____

_____

_____

_____

Emerge

Action Taking Exercise: Spend time outside in the same spot as before, near water, if possible, to sit silently in prayer. Ask God to open your heart again, to allow the feeling of compassion and hope to fill it once more. Use this space to jot down anything that comes to your mind while you complete this exercise.

_____

_____

_____

_____

_____

_____

_____

_____

_____

_____

Dedicate

Being compassionate towards others means to me...

_____

_____

_____

_____

_____

_____

_____

_____

_____

_____

_____

_____

_____

_____

_____

_____

Declaration Statements

"I am" statement: Write a statement about who you feel you are in this very moment. *Example: I am never alone.*

I am

_____

_____

"I hope to be" statement: Write a statement about who you hope to be by the end of this book. *Example: I hope to be closer to God.*

I hope to be

_____

_____

Chapter Four
Seeing the Beauty in God's Design

In hardship, we often hastily grab the reigns that control which direction we are headed and gallop blindly at full speed. When we live life in this fast paced way, we may miss out on the beautiful life God has designed for us. As you work on handing the reigns over to God, I want to encourage you that it will be okay. One thing I struggled with was the feeling of unworthiness I carried because I had chosen to walk away from God as I struggled forward on the rockiest path I had ever endured. With every stumble, I was determined to figure out how to get back on a smoother path. By inviting God to join you where you are in the rocky terrain, He will help guide you back towards the path He has beautifully crafted for you to walk. He will never leave your side, no matter how tumultuous the path may become.

Affirm

Scripture Memorization: Write the following scripture and post it somewhere you'll see it every day. Maybe it's a bathroom mirror, refrigerator, or your home office. Memorize it and refer to it when you feel alone at the bottom of the ocean.

"Trust in the Lord with all your heart and lean not on your own understanding; in all your ways submit to him, and he will make your paths straight."—Proverbs 3:5–6

Notate

Scripture Application: Reading the verse in Proverbs 3:5-6, how can this verse be applied to your life today?

_____

_____

_____

_____

_____

_____

Craft

Creative Exercise: Rough sketch a road below that starts at the bottom and goes up and off the page at the top, showing an open unending road. Using any coloring medium (crayons, pencils, etc.), add different terrains that depict your journey leading up to this moment. Start at the bottom of the road and end halfway through your road. If your journey had rocky times, be sure to add in the rocks to depict that part of your journey. At the halfway mark, add a directional sign pointing up to the end of your road with one word written on it that captures the hope you have for your future. On the upper half of the road, add colorful flowers and grass along the sides of the road and put something in the middle of the road that represents God leading you forward.

Honor

Prayer: *Heavenly Father, thank you for reminding me that you have already paved the way for me. Life has been hard, I have been hurt and let down, and my path has been so very rocky and doesn't align with what I had hoped it would. I'm tired and frustrated, I feel like I'm not getting to where I need to be going, and I don't know what to do next. I give up my control to you, Lord, and humbly ask that you lead me down the path you have before me. Thank you, Lord, for the beauty that awaits me, Amen.*

Observe

- **Exercise:** Find a place where you can sit in silence and solitude. Sit somewhere comfortably and put your right hand over your heart. Breathe deeply in and out for a count of 10. Ask God to remind you of any beautiful moments in your life as you sit in silence.
- **Journal:** Write down anything that comes to mind, your first thought, the moments that come to you, and any details you can remember.

When you have reached a point of no more thoughts, give thanks to God for helping you remember the joy.

_____

_____

_____

_____

_____

_____

_____

_____

_____

_____

_____

Rebuild

Using your road photo, looking back on your life up until this point, does it look how you had hoped it would? Why or why not?

_____

_____

_____

_____

_____

_____

_____

Can you find any moments in time that feel like a lesson was to be learned? What is the moment and what is God telling you about that moment?

_____

_____

_____

_____

_____

_____

_____

The path I've traveled up to this point looks like…

_____

_____

_____

_____

_____

_____

_____

Emerge

Action Taking Exercise: Spend time outside in the same spot as before, near water, if possible, to sit silently in prayer. Ask God to provide you with a sense of peace and understanding. Acknowledge how you feel about the path your road has taken you on up until this point, and admit to God any frustrations, disappointments, or heartaches caused by the unexpected twists and turns. Surrender to God, giving it all to Him to carry, and thank Him for lightening your heavy load. Use this space to jot down anything that comes to your mind while you complete this exercise.

_____

_____

_____

_____

_____

_____

_____

_____

_____

_____

_____

_____

_____

_____

_____

_____

_____

_____

_____

Dedicate

Seeking God's direction in my life first looks like..

_____

_____

_____

_____

_____

One thing I need to do to shift my perspective to start seeing the beauty in God's design for my life is:

_____

_____

_____

_____

_____

_____

Declaration Statements

"I am" statement: Write a statement about who you feel you are in this very moment. *Example: I am on a detour.*

I am

_____

_____

"I hope to be" statement: Write a statement about who you hope to be by the end of this book. *Example: I hope to be able to see the beauty in God's design for my life.*

I hope to be

_____

_____

Chapter Five
Rebuilding Friendship

Having someone you can lean on when times get tough helps us to get through to brighter days. When it comes to rebuilding your friendships, knowing the characteristics you bring and how they pair with those of others will help you determine who you choose to lean on during trying times. You want someone who not only helps build you up but who you feel comfortable helping build them up as well. Throughout these exercises, pray that God places the names on your heart of those He wants you to rebuild a friendship with.

Affirm

Scripture Memorization: Write the following scripture and post it somewhere you'll see it every day. Maybe it's a bathroom mirror, refrigerator, or your home office. Memorize it and refer to it when you feel alone at the bottom of the ocean.

"Therefore encourage one another and build each other up, just as in fact you are doing."—1 Thessalonians 5:11

Notate

Scripture Application: Reading the verse in 1 Thessalonians 5:11, how can this verse be applied to your life today?

_____

_____

_____

_____

_____

_____

_____

_____

_____

_____

Craft

Creative Exercise: Draw a picture of a tree with many roots going down into the ground. Where each root is, write in a characteristic of genuine friendship that comes to mind.

Honor

Prayer: *Heavenly Father, thank you for helping me discover the vulnerabilities in friendship I carry with me. I realize I may have kept my friends at arm's length apart to guard my heart, and I ask that you help me to learn to let them in again. I pray, Lord, for my person, that you make them known to me and help me to nurture and grow that relationship into a deep-rooted relationship that lasts for a very long time. Thank you, Lord, for the friendship that awaits me, Amen.*

Observe

- **Exercise:** On a sheet of paper, write out the names of every relationship you've developed over the years that were at one point significant and meaningful (friends, family, foe).
  - Use a red pen to circle the names of those whom you've fallen out of connection with for one reason or another.
  - Use a blue pen to circle anyone who is family.
  - Use a green pen to circle anyone who is still a friend.
  - Once you've circled all the names on your list, use the red pen to cross out any names of individuals whose connection is irreparable; meaning you cannot repair that relationship due to the severity of the connection break or due to the passing of the person.
  - Use the blue pen to put a heart next to the family members who are still supporting and encouraging you today.
  - Use the green pen to put a leaf next to the friendships that are still active—even if it's a small interaction—or ones you hope to rebuild.
- **Journal:** Looking at your list and focusing on the leaves, write about 3 individuals you hope to deepen a connection with and why you want to rebuild.

Individual 1

_____

_____

_____

_____

Individual 2

_____

_____

_____

_____

Individual 3

_____

_____

_____

_____

Rebuild

Looking at your tree picture, write about which of those genuine friendship characteristics you bring to your friendships.

_____

_____

_____

_____

_____

_____

_____

Looking at your tree picture, write about which of those genuine friendship characteristics mean the most to you from a friend and why those are important to you.

_____

_____

_____

_____

_____

_____

_____

The vulnerabilities I have that I need to address are…

_____

_____

_____

_____

_____

_____

_____

Emerge

Action Taking Exercise: Pick someone from your list that you either feel a strong connection with still or once did and hope to rebuild. Send them a greeting card in the mail with a handwritten note letting them know you are thinking of them and how much they mean to you. Use this space to jot down anything that comes to your mind while you complete this exercise.

_____

_____

_____

_____

_____

_____

_____

_____

_____

_____

_____

_____

_____

_____

Dedicate

Thinking of the person you chose to send the card to, write out ways you can work on strengthening that relationship with them and what characteristics from your tree you need to incorporate into your friendship.

_____
_____
_____
_____
_____
_____
_____
_____
_____
_____
_____
_____
_____
_____

Declaration Statements

"I am" statement: Write a statement about who you feel you are in this very moment. _Example: I am hopeful._

I am

_____
_____

"I hope to be" statement: Write a statement about who you hope to be by the end of this book. _Example: I hope to be confident in my identity._

I hope to be

_____
_____

Chapter Six
Rediscover Your Passions

Allowing yourself to tap into your inner child when looking at potential hobbies will help you be more open to new possibilities that you may have written off without giving them a chance. It still may or may not work, but at least you'll have tried. Move freely when testing new potentials, take note of how they make you feel as you test it out. Did they bring you happiness or fill your heart with gladness? Those are the activities you'll want to repeat on days that are hard.

Affirm

Scripture Memorization: Write the following scripture and post it somewhere you'll see it every day. Maybe it's a bathroom mirror, refrigerator, or your home office. Memorize it and refer to it when you feel alone at the bottom of the ocean.

"For we are God's handiwork, created in Christ Jesus to do good works, which God prepared in advance for us to do." —Ephesians 2:10

Notate

Scripture Application: Reading the verse in Ephesians 2:10, how can this verse be applied to your life today?

_____
_____
_____
_____
_____
_____
_____
_____
_____
_____

Craft

Creative Exercise: Anything goes! This is the chance for you to dive into a passion or hobby you haven't picked up in a long time. Is it coloring? Painting? Cross-stitch? Photography? Writing? Reading? Hiking? Dancing? If you have never really found a hobby that resonated with you, pick something new to try. Use this space to jot down anything that comes to your mind while you completed this exercise.

_____

_____

_____

_____

_____

_____

_____

_____

_____

_____

_____

_____

_____

_____

_____

Honor

Prayer: *Heavenly Father, thank you for reminding me of the things that once brought me joy. I ask, Lord, that you help me see what skills or gifts you have blessed me with. Please make known to me how you want me to use them to help someone else in need. I haven't always felt valuable, Lord, and I see now that I can and do bring value to those around me. I want to rediscover my passions in a new light, your light. Thank you, Lord, for the joy that awaits me, Amen.*

Observe

- **Exercise:** Passion Mapping

What activities make you lose track of time and feel fully submerged in the moment?

_____
_____
_____

When you were a child, what did you enjoy doing for fun or as a hobby?

_____
_____
_____

What talents or skills do your friends and family compliment you on?

_____
_____
_____

Is there a specific cause, issue, or topic that you're passionate about?

_____
_____
_____

What types of books, movies, or art keep your attention the most? Why?

_____
_____
_____
_____
_____

Have you ever started a project or hobby and found it difficult to stop because you were so into it? What made it difficult to stop?

_____

_____

_____

_____

_____

_____

What dreams or aspirations keep coming up in your mind, even if you haven't pursued them yet?

_____

_____

_____

_____

Are there any activities or hobbies you've always wanted to try but never had the time or means to?

_____

_____

_____

What activities or interests align with your values and beliefs?

_____

_____

_____

If time and money were not constraints, how would you spend your days?

_____

_____

_____

_____

- **Journal:** Rediscover your passions by using your answers in the Passion Mapping Exercise.

The passions and/or hobbies I once had that brought me joy were...

_____
_____
_____
_____
_____
_____
_____
_____

The common hobby or interest that was revealed to me during my passion mapping is...

_____
_____
_____
_____
_____
_____
_____
_____

What are ways I can begin incorporating this hobby/interest in my life starting now?

_____
_____
_____
_____
_____
_____
_____
_____

Rebuild

One thing that really brings me joy when I am doing it is...

_____

_____

_____

_____

I feel my best on hard days when I...

_____

_____

_____

_____

Emerge

Action Taking Exercise: Test drive the hobby/interest you discovered during your passion mapping. Use any resources you may already have, or if you don't have what you need, spend this time researching ways to get started that fit with your lifestyle. If the hobby/interest you landed on is out of reach due to finances, I encourage you to seek alternative ways to get started, online is a great place to research ways to do this more budget friendly. (YouTube and/or Pinterest) Use this space to jot down anything that comes to your mind while you complete this exercise.

_____

_____

_____

_____

_____

_____

_____

_____

_____

Dedicate

How do I feel about getting started with this hobby (again or for the first time)?

_____

_____

_____

_____

_____

_____

_____

_____

_____

_____

_____

_____

_____

_____

_____

Declaration Statements

"I am" statement: Write a statement about who you feel you are in this very moment. *Example: I am a graphic designer.*

I am

_____

_____

"I hope to be" statement: Write a statement about who you hope to be by the end of this book. *Example: I hope to be able to share my design skills with others to bring them joy while glorifying God.*

I hope to be

_____

_____

Chapter Seven

Forced to Pivot

change doesn't have to be scary. It's ok to stop running and face your changes head on with God by your side. I want to encourage you to seek out the positives that accompany this change. It may be difficult to do at first, but with time, patience, and practice, you'll be able to find at least one positive that comes from change.

Affirm

Scripture Memorization: Write the following scripture and post it somewhere you'll see it every day. Maybe it's a bathroom mirror, refrigerator, or your home office. Memorize it and refer to it when you feel alone at the bottom of the ocean.

"Here I am! I stand at the door and knock. If anyone hears my voice and opens the door, I will come in and eat with that person, and they with me." —Revelations 3:20

Notate

Scripture Application: Reading the verse in Revelation 3:20, how can this verse be applied to your life today?

_____

_____

_____

_____

_____

_____

_____

_____

_____

_____

_____

Craft

Mirror Exercise: Look into the mirror, lock eyes with yourself, and ask "What now?" Allow those fears and insecurities to creep in, and then pivot your mindset into that of an encourager. What would you tell a friend going through this unexpected challenge? Speak words of encouragement to the woman in the mirror. Use this space to jot down anything that comes to your mind while you completed this exercise.

_____

_____

_____

_____

_____

_____

_____

_____

_____

_____

Honor

Prayer: *Heavenly Father, thank you for your patience in me and in my disobedience. It is never my intent to do the opposite of what you ask. Please help me, Lord, to have the strength and courage to go where you lead me. Lord, please quiet the noise within my mind so that I may hear your call at the door as you knock. Please give me the strength to open the door and step through it to what awaits me on the other side. Thank you, Lord, for believing in me when others haven't, Amen.*

Observe

- **Exercise:** Stand at your front door inside your home, looking at the door as it is closed. Think about your situation and the need to pivot to continue forward. There is a closed door standing between you and reaching your goal. Take note of how you feel thinking about this and come back to journal about it.

- **Journal:** Thinking back to your time at the front door, answer these questions.

What is on the other side of that door?

_____

_____

_____

_____

_____

What is on the other side of the door that scares me?

_____

_____

_____

_____

_____

- **Exercise:** Back at your front door, close your eyes and picture Jesus on the other side of the door waiting on you. Open your eyes, look at the closed door, and take a deep breath. Release your breath and then open your front door and step out. Look around. What do you see, what do you hear, and what do you feel? Take note of everything and come back to journal about it.
- **Journal:** Thinking back to your time on the other side of your front door, answer this question.

How did I feel once I walked through my front door and outside?

_____

_____

_____

_____

_____

Rebuild

Write about a time when you found yourself needing to pivot. How did that situation make you feel?

_____

_____

_____

_____

Are you currently in a situation that is causing you to have to make changes?

_____

_____

_____

_____

Emerge

Action Taking Exercise: A new plan is needed for you to get back on track with your goals. Take time to reflect on your current goals.

_____

_____

_____

_____

_____

Write down your long-term goals even if they feel out of reach.

_____

_____

_____

_____

_____

_____

Review your goals and consider which ones align with God's plan for you and which may need adjustments. Make any adjustments you feel are needed. Write out the top three goals in both sections that come up during this process as you reflect on God's plan for you.

Short-term goals

1.

2.

3.

Long-term goals

1.

2.

3.

Dedicate

As I was writing out my long term goals, I felt a new focus should be on…

_____

_____

_____

_____

_____

_____

_____

_____

_____

_____

_____

_____

_____

_____

Declaration Statements

"I am" statement: Write a statement about who you feel you are in this very moment. *Example: I am scared to walk through the door that awaits me.*

I am

_____

_____

"I hope to be" statement: Write a statement about who you hope to be by the end of this book. *Example: I hope to be a messenger for God.*

I hope to be

_____

_____

Chapter Eight
Autopilot

Do you feel like you are living on autopilot as you do the same things over and over, day in and day out? It's easy to fall into this pattern and get stuck in it for quite some time. It can be overwhelming to think about breaking free from this monotony, but it isn't impossible. All you must do is take that first step and keep going.

Affirm

Scripture Memorization: Write the following scripture and post it somewhere you'll see it every day. Maybe it's a bathroom mirror, refrigerator, or your home office. Memorize it and refer to it when you feel alone at the bottom of the ocean.

"Teach us to number our days, that we may gain a heart of wisdom." —Psalm 90:12

Notate

Scripture Application: Reading the verse in Psalm 90:12, how can this verse be applied to your life today?

_____
_____
_____
_____
_____
_____
_____
_____
_____
_____
_____
_____

Craft

Fifteen-Minute Timer Exercise: Your to-do list is likely overwhelming, but what I want to encourage you to do right now is pick one thing on your to-do list, set a timer for fifteen minutes, and work only on that one task. When the timer goes off, you are done, even if the task isn't completed.

Honor

Prayer: *Heavenly Father, thank you for helping me recognize the importance of living a life filled with intent and purpose alongside of you. I pray, Lord, and ask that you help me to see my life through your eyes, help me to know when I am living on autopilot, and help me to trust you to bring me through it. I pray, Lord, for strength as I face each new day, and the courage to take action fifteen minutes at a time. Thank you, Lord, for being my pilot and helping me to see life in a whole new light, Amen.*

Observe

- **Time Audit Exercise:** Where am I spending my time? Write out time in sixty-minute increments for one day from the moment you wake up until the time you go to sleep.
    - Fill in your non-negotiable/fixed-in-time events in each time slot it is already set in. Example: Dinner every day at 5:30 pm–6:30 pm; Work 8–12, Lunch 12–1, Work 1–5, etc.
    - Add in the moments you hope to do every day. Example: Prayer/study, self-care, TV time, etc.
    - I highly recommend morning time as faith time, if possible, to start your day with God. I have personally made this a non-negotiable time slot daily.
    - Using highlighters or colored pens, assign a color to groupings by adding a colored dot next to the time you've set. Example: Pink = self-care; Blue = family; Green = work; Purple = faith
    - This sets up your basic time blocking schedule and gives you a quick glance at where your time is being allocated.

Time Blocking

5 AM	
6 AM	
7 AM	
8 AM	
9 AM	
10 AM	
11 AM	
12 PM	
1 PM	
2 PM	
3 PM	
4 PM	
5 PM	
6 PM	
7 PM	
8 PM	
9 PM	
10 PM	
11 PM	

- **Journal:** Look over your time blocking and answer the following questions.

What surprises me the most about where my time is being allocated?

_____

_____

_____

_____

_____

_____

_____

_____

Are there any times in my day not accounted for that I could add in a hobby or other thing that brings me joy?

_____

_____

_____

_____

_____

_____

_____

_____

My biggest takeaway from seeing where my time is being spent is...

_____

_____

_____

_____

_____

_____

_____

Rebuild

How do I feel about getting (some of) my tasks completed?

_____

_____

_____

_____

How many fifteen-minute timers would it take to complete the task I started?

_____

_____

_____

_____

Realistically, how much time can I devote daily to work on tasks in fifteen-minute increments?

_____

_____

_____

_____

Emerge

Action Taking Exercise: Set a fifteen-minute timer. Take the next fifteen minutes to either work on the task from the to-do list you originally created or pick a new task on your list that needs to be worked on. Only work on this task during your fifteen-minute timer. Use this space to jot down anything that comes to your mind while you completed this exercise.

_____

_____

_____

_____

_____

Dedicate

What does "Be a good steward of your time" mean to me, and how can I apply it to my time management?

_____

_____

_____

_____

_____

_____

As I look around my house, I see reflections of the state my mind is in and what I am seeing is...

_____

_____

_____

_____

_____

Declaration Statements

"I am" statement: Write a statement about who you feel you are in this very moment. _Example: I am exhausted._

I am

_____

_____

"I hope to be" statement: Write a statement about who you hope to be by the end of this book. _Example: I hope to be a good steward of my time and home._

I hope to be

_____

_____

Chapter Nine
Life Has a Meaning

Your life has meaning, and you have a purpose. I had a hard time accepting that I could have a purpose outside of my circumstances, but I have learned that God created me to help others. Even during trials, you can discover God's plan for you by looking for purpose in your struggles.

Affirm

Scripture Memorization: Write the following scripture and post it somewhere you'll see it every day. Maybe it's a bathroom mirror, refrigerator, or your home office. Memorize it and refer to it when you feel alone at the bottom of the ocean.

"'I am the Lord's servant,' Mary answered. May your word to me be fulfilled."
—Luke 1:38

Notate

Scripture Application: Reading the verse in Luke 1:38, how can this verse be applied to your life today?

_____

_____

_____

_____

_____

_____

_____

_____

_____

_____

_____

Craft

Creative Exercise: Have you ever felt called to do something that you are currently not doing?

- Use the provided line that extends across the paper. The beginning of the line should be dated with the first memory you have of when you felt like you should be doing something (called) but maybe didn't do it. The end of the line should be left undated.
- Thinking back over your life, add date points on your line for when this calling was made present in your life at additional times. If you fulfilled the calling, add the date you answered the call to your line. If you have not yet fulfilled the calling or are unsure if it is a calling, try to uncover how many times this thought or idea came to mind and made itself known to you.
- The top of the line is where you put the date, the bottom of the line is where you list specifics to your calling.

Honor

Prayer: *Heavenly Father, thank you for believing in me even with all that I have gone through. Lord, I know you have been calling me to do something, but I often let fear win and dismiss the thought before it has the chance to take root. Lord, I ask that you please make known to me your purpose and plan for my life, help me to see and know the signs you place before me. Thank you, Lord, for choosing me to help others find their way to your kingdom, Amen.*

Observe

- **Exercise:** List out some experiences and skills you possess that you believe could be connected to your calling.

Experiences	Skills

- **Journal:** Refer back to your list of experiences and skills when answering the following questions.

How has God equipped me during times of resistance or denial?

_____

_____

_____

_____

_____

_____

_____

Are there any specific areas or ministries where I feel a strong pull or connection?

_____

_____

_____

_____

_____

_____

_____

Looking back at everything I have gone through; I feel my lessons are...

_____

_____

_____

_____

_____

_____

_____

Rebuild

Have I ever felt a strong inner calling or sense of purpose?

_____

_____

_____

_____

Have I resisted or denied this calling in the past? Why?

_____

_____

_____

_____

Emerge

Action Taking Exercise: Write down steps you can take to begin or continue your journey toward fulfilling your calling. Take a picture or make a copy and put this someplace where you can see it daily. Optional: add a goal date to answer your call.

Step One   Goal Date:

Step Two   Goal Date:

Step Three   Goal Date:

Dedicate

Write about your calling, listing any thoughts that come to mind.

_____

_____

_____

_____

_____

_____

_____

_____

_____

_____

_____

_____

_____

_____

_____

_____

_____

Declaration Statements

"I am" statement: Write a statement about who you feel you are in this very moment. _Example: I am chosen._

I am

_____

_____

"I hope to be" statement: Write a statement about who you hope to be by the end of this book. _Example: I hope to be a beacon of light for others in need._

I hope to be

_____

_____

Chapter Ten
Change is Hard

Change can be challenging, but it's necessary for growth. God wants us to get up, take action, and work towards our goals and aspirations. If you are hesitant or unsure of yourself and your capabilities, the best way to become sure is to do all you can to learn and grow in the areas you have uncertainty.

Affirm

Scripture Memorization: Write the following scripture and post it somewhere you'll see it every day. Maybe it's a bathroom mirror, refrigerator, or your home office. Memorize it and refer to it when you feel alone at the bottom of the ocean.

"Commit to the Lord whatever you do and he will establish your plans." — Proverbs 16:3

Notate

Scripture Application: Reading the verse in Proverbs 16:3, how can this verse be applied to your life today?

_____

_____

_____

_____

_____

_____

_____

_____

_____

_____

_____

_____

Craft

Mirror Exercise: Look at yourself in the mirror (lock eyes); think of all the limiting beliefs you have about yourself. For me, it was that I was uneducated, not good enough, fat, etc.

- Using a dry erase marker or post it notes, write the opposite of what you believe to be true and place it on the mirror around your reflection so when you look in the mirror every day you see these new truths
  - Uneducated = experienced
  - Not good enough = qualified
  - Fat = healthy
  - Every day, read them out loud with confidence and an "I am" statement before them.
  - I am experienced!
- Leave these new truths up until you begin to believe them, and then as you remove one, put a new one up; go at your pace, some of these took several months for me to fully believe before I could take them down.

Honor

Prayer: *Heavenly Father, thank you for the hard lessons you've brought me through and the reminder that you were with me through it all. Lord, I know I haven't been true to myself or you. I ask that you help me uncover the negativities in my life that need to be transformed into positivities. Please give me the strength to face each of these areas head on so I can begin to conquer them one by one as I start to move forward again. Thank you, Lord, for waiting patiently on me, Amen.*

Observe

- **Exercise:** If you are on social media: Share a selfie of you today and in your caption include the following: "I am proud of who I am."Feel free to elaborate or simply keep this statement. (Feel free to tag me in it; I would love to share your post!)
- **Exercise:** If you aren't on social media: Take a selfie, open it in a photo editor, and write on it (but not over your face), "I am proud of who I am." Save it and look at it often.

- **Journal:** Reflect on the way you felt during the mirror exercise and the selfie exercise.

What is one thing you are proud of yourself for doing?

_____

_____

_____

_____

_____

_____

_____

_____

_____

_____

_____

Rebuild

What do I believe is the root cause of my limiting beliefs?

_____

_____

_____

_____

_____

_____

_____

_____

_____

_____

_____

_____

What is one thing I recognize I need to change about my mindset?

_____

_____

_____

_____

_____

_____

Emerge

Action Taking Exercise: Plan out action steps to take to answer a calling you currently have. I like to give myself a realistic deadline so that I can stay on task and reach the goal. If you aren't quite ready to answer fully, it is okay to have your action steps be smaller and lead up to the bigger ones.

☐ _____

☐ _____

☐ _____

☐ _____

☐ _____

☐ _____

☐ _____

☐ _____

☐ _____

☐ _____

☐ _____

☐ _____

☐ _____

☐ _____

Dedicate

One area that I have become most negative and need to change is…

_____

_____

_____

_____

_____

_____

Even though change can be scary, I am most excited about the chance to…

_____

_____

_____

_____

_____

_____

Declaration Statements

"I am" statement: Write a statement about who you feel you are in this very moment. *Example: I am qualified.*

I am

_____

_____

"I hope to be" statement: Write a statement about who you hope to be by the end of this book. *Example: I hope to be a good leader for God's kingdom.*

I hope to be

_____

_____

Chapter Eleven
Paint Chips = Progress

When it comes to measuring our progress, we default to putting such high expectations on ourselves that our goals may become unattainable. Celebrate any level of progress you make as you move forward. It isn't expected that you are going to knock it out of the park on a homerun hit the first time out. Sometimes progress is as simple as picking up a stack of paint chips.

Affirm

Scripture Memorization: Write the following scripture and post it somewhere you'll see it every day. Maybe it's a bathroom mirror, refrigerator, or your home office. Memorize it and refer to it when you feel alone at the bottom of the ocean.

"So whether you eat or drink or whatever you do, do it all for the glory of God."
—1 Corinthians 10:31

Notate

Scripture Application: Reading the verse in 1 Corinthians 10:31, how can this verse be applied to your life today?

_____

_____

_____

_____

_____

_____

_____

_____

_____

_____

_____

Craft

Creative Exercise: Use colored pencils to make this Gift Certificate bright and cheery. Add your name on the "To:" line. Once you've completed these steps, move forward until prompted to come back to it again.

Gift Certificate

To: _____

For: _____

From the bottom of my heart, I Want to:

_____

_____

_____

_____   _____
Signature   Expires

Honor

Prayer: *Heavenly Father, thank you for the reminder that even ordinary everyday activities can be done in a way that brings honor to you. On days when I feel like I haven't done enough, please remind me that even the smallest act I make is enough. Thank you, Lord, for helping me work through change and step out more in faith, Amen.*

Observe

- **Journal:** Option 1: Gift of Talent: Take time to consider your gifts and talents.

How could you use your gifts to help someone else who would benefit from your unique talents?

_____

_____

_____

_____

_____

_____

_____

_____

Who comes to mind when you think of helping someone?

_____

_____

_____

_____

_____

_____

_____

_____

- **Journal:** Option 2: Gift of Progress (Time): Take time to consider areas you have been struggling with that need your attention.

Write down the things you have not had energy or motivation to do, but have wanted to do for quite some time. Pick one that feels manageable with a little bit of planning. What amount of time will it take to accomplish this task?

_____

_____

_____

_____

_____

_____

_____

_____

_____

_____

What steps will you take to progress forward by taking care of this task that you have been putting off?

_____

_____

_____

_____

_____

_____

_____

_____

_____

_____

_____

- **Exercise:** You will need to go back to the gift certificate you crafted earlier and the journal entries you wrote during this observation. It is time to pick one of these options and commit to taking the next step toward progress.
  - Fill in the blanks of your gift certificate with the pertinent information.
    - The "For:" line should include your offering—be specific to what the task is.
    - Write out a message from the heart with why you are willing to do this now.
    - The date of expiration should be the date you are committing to completing the task.
    - Lastly, sign the final blank line to lock in your commitment.
  - Take a photograph of your gift certificate and keep it somewhere you will see it every day as a reminder of your commitment to the deadline you've set.

Rebuild

Thinking back to the certificate you made, write out a plan of action to fulfill your commitment.

_____

_____

_____

_____

_____

_____

_____

_____

Give yourself permission to be transparent—how do you feel about making this commitment?

_____

_____

_____

_____

_____

_____

_____

_____

One way I can see I am making progress is...

_____

_____

_____

_____

_____

_____

_____

_____

_____

_____

_____

_____

_____

_____

_____

Emerge

Action Taking Exercise: Declaration of intent—Real talk. One thing that I learned about myself was that often, good intentions would fall to the wayside if only I knew about them. Not having the accountability offered me the opportunity to not do the hard thing I said I would do. It's so easy to fall into this trap. That is why declaring your intent to someone else will breathe life into your commitment. What I would like for you to do is go to your person (or a trusted friend/colleague) and share with them the commitment you made. Let them know what your timeline is and ask them to help hold you accountable to fulfilling this commitment and to keep you in their prayers as you step out and make progress. If you cannot think of anyone who you feel would help you, I invite you to reach out in our Facebook Group, I will cheer you on! You are so brave for making this commitment!

You can access the group at: www.facebook.com/groups/authenticallyanchored

Dedicate

How do I feel about giving all that I have to put into my commitment?

_____

_____

_____

_____

_____

What fears are coming to surface after making this commitment?

_____

_____

_____

_____

_____

_____

Declaration Statements

"I am" statement: Write a statement about who you feel you are in this very moment. *Example: I am making some progress.*

I am

_____

_____

"I hope to be" statement: Write a statement about who you hope to be by the end of this book. *Example: I hope to be more consistent in honoring God in all that I do.*

I hope to be

_____

_____

Chapter Twelve
It's Going to Be Okay

Despite life's challenges, everything will be okay. You can find peace and acceptance in your circumstances by drawing into your faith and trusting God's plan. It's okay to get back out there and try again. You are so brave and strong!

Affirm

Scripture Memorization: Write the following scripture and post it somewhere you'll see it every day. Maybe it's a bathroom mirror, refrigerator, or your home office. Memorize it and refer to it when you feel alone at the bottom of the ocean.

"You make known to me the path of life; you will fill me with joy in your presence, with eternal pleasures at your right hand." —Psalm 16:11

Notate

Scripture Application: Reading the verse in Psalm 16:11, how can this verse be applied to your life today?

_____

_____

_____

_____

_____

_____

_____

_____

_____

_____

_____

_____

_____

_____

Craft

Mirror Exercise: Lock eyes with yourself in the mirror. Take a few deep breaths to relax, inhale through your nose and exhale through your mouth. While maintaining eye contact with yourself, repeat the following statement over and over for as long as you need, no less than 10 times: "I am confident and capable." Use this space to jot down anything that comes to your mind while you complete this exercise.

_____

_____

_____

_____

_____

_____

_____

_____

_____

_____

_____

_____

_____

_____

_____

_____

_____

Honor

Prayer: *Heavenly Father, I am often afraid and filled with feelings of anxiousness or worry that steal my peace. Thank you for the reminder that no matter what, no matter who I am, it's going to be ok. Lord, please help me to be brave as I lean into the possibility of becoming more my authentic self in you. Thank you, Lord, for helping me slay the giants before me, Amen.*

Observe

- **Mirror Exercise:** Lock eyes with yourself in the mirror and maintain eye contact throughout this exercise. Take a few deep breaths to relax, inhale through your nose and exhale through your mouth. Repeat the following statement over and over for as long as you need, no less than 10 times: "I believe in myself and my abilities."
- **Journal:** Believing in yourself and your abilities.

Something(s) that someone incorrectly told me I was incapable of doing, is:

_____

_____

_____

_____

_____

_____

_____

_____

_____

I am capable of doing

_____

Because of (fill in your abilities)

_____

I am capable of doing

_____

Because of (fill in your abilities)

_____

Rebuild

What does "I am confident and capable" look like on me? (Visualize yourself in this state.)

_____
_____
_____
_____
_____
_____
_____
_____
_____
_____
_____
_____
_____
_____

I desire to be living in peace, therefore I will let go of…

_____
_____
_____
_____
_____
_____
_____
_____
_____
_____
_____
_____
_____

Emerge

Action Taking Exercise: Take a notebook or journal with you outside, near water if possible, sit and think back to all the times you were told you couldn't or you shouldn't. It's important during this time to not get stuck in the negative of those moments, but rather, look deeper into your truth. Perhaps someone judged your abilities without fully knowing what you are capable of, or maybe they didn't give you a fair chance. Write down the missed opportunities you had—focus on the what, not the who.

_____

_____

_____

_____

_____

_____

_____

_____

_____

_____

_____

_____

_____

_____

_____

_____

I want you to now look over your list and pick one area to focus on, this should be the one missed opportunity that you think of the most and wish you could have proven your capabilities. For me, it was in web design, that I missed the opportunity to prove my skills due to lack of confidence. I want you to now write down a brainstorm of ideas on how you can turn it into a learning experience for your growth. Because I regretted not being able to show my capabilities in web design, I began studying it more in-depth and practiced on many different platforms further enhancing my skills.

Brainstorm

From a missed opportunity to a season of growth.

_____

_____

_____

_____

_____

_____

_____

_____

_____

_____

_____

_____

_____

_____

_____

_____

_____

_____

_____

_____

_____

_____

_____

_____

Dedicate

Thinking back to your area of focus in the last exercise, what can you do to become more confident in your skills, so you don't have another missed opportunity? Perhaps your skill doesn't need to be improved upon but rather the courage to stand up for yourself in the face of doubt. Write about it.

_____

_____

_____

_____

_____

_____

_____

_____

_____

_____

_____

_____

_____

Declaration Statements

"I am" statement: Write a statement about who you feel you are in this very moment. *Example: I am confident and capable.*

I am

_____

_____

"I hope to be" statement: Write a statement about who you hope to be by the end of this book. *Example: I hope to be my most authentic self always, without fear.*

I hope to be

_____

_____

Chapter Thirteen
Love Yourself as God Loves You

How do you feel about loving yourself as a beautiful creation of God? The first time someone asked me that, I am certain I rolled my eyes. Loving myself wasn't something I could just do, I had to work in this area for quite some time. Let go of feeling like you don't matter, and start looking at yourself through the eyes of the Lord.

Affirm

Scripture Memorization: Write the following scripture and post it somewhere you'll see it every day. Maybe it's a bathroom mirror, refrigerator, or your home office. Memorize it and refer to it when you feel alone at the bottom of the ocean.

"Do you not know that your bodies are temples of the Holy Spirit, who is in you, whom you have received from God? You are not your own; you were bought at a price. Therefore, honor God with your bodies." —1 Corinthians 6:19–20

Notate

Scripture Application: Reading the verse in 1 Corinthians 6:19-20, how can this verse be applied to your life today?

_____

_____

_____

_____

_____

_____

_____

_____

_____

_____

_____

Craft

Creative Exercise: Draw a self-portrait that showcases your unique qualities (both inner and outer).

Honor

Prayer: *Heavenly Father, I am so sorry for not loving myself as you love me. I have struggled to see what you see in me and have allowed the opinions of others to keep me captive in my mind. Lord, I ask for your help as I try harder to honor my temple so that I can honor you. Thank you, Lord, for giving me the strength to keep trying, Amen.*

Observe

- **Exercise:** Using a blank piece of paper, spend time somewhere comfortable and quiet where you won't be interrupted. Write a letter to yourself, expressing your love and appreciation for yourself just as you would for someone you deeply care about. Once you've written it, fold it and put it somewhere you will come across it when you need it most.
- **Journal:** Think back to how you felt when writing your letter.

When writing the love letter to yourself, how hard was it for you to write with compassion for yourself? Why do you think that is?

_____

_____

_____

_____

_____

_____

_____

_____

_____

_____

_____

_____

Rebuild

Write about 3 things you appreciate about yourself. Be specific, detailed, and thoughtful in your approach.

_____

_____

_____

_____

_____

_____

_____

_____

_____

_____

_____

The way God has shown me how much he loves me is...

_____

_____

_____

_____

_____

_____

_____

_____

_____

_____

_____

_____

Emerge

Action Taking Exercise: You need some time in thought and prayer on this topic, I want to encourage you to first create a playlist (if you don't already have one) that inspires you. You can also use the Authentically Anchored Spotify Playlist mentioned in the introduction of this book. Gather your headphones and phone, put on your walking shoes, and head outside. Your goal right now is to walk to a minimum of 3 songs, if possible. During this time, I want you to think about your temple (body) and how you are or are not honoring it. What are some areas of improvement for your overall health that you recognize? What are ways you could give yourself grace when it comes to how you speak to yourself (or think)? Lastly, I want you to pray for God's guidance in this area, self-love is an area I have personally struggled with for a long time. Ask God to open your heart to allow yourself to love who you are in HIM. When you have reached the end of song 3 you can head back in, or stay out for as long as you wish, that choice is yours to make. Use this space to jot down anything that comes to your mind while you complete this exercise.

_____

_____

_____

_____

_____

_____

_____

_____

_____

_____

_____

_____

_____

_____

_____

_____

_____

Dedicate

While on my walk, the things I realized are:

_____

_____

_____

_____

_____

_____

I really want to start honoring my temple by:

_____

_____

_____

_____

_____

_____

_____

_____

Declaration Statements

"I am" statement: Write a statement about who you feel you are in this very moment. *Example: I am strong and determined.*

I am

_____

_____

"I hope to be" statement: Write a statement about who you hope to be by the end of this book. *Example: I hope to be kinder to my temple.*

I hope to be

_____

_____

Chapter Fourteen
(Re)Build Your Community

We are not meant to be alone in life, having a community of like minded individuals is helpful for us. Building a supportive community is vital for personal growth. Reconnect with others and offer support and encouragement to one another. I want to encourage you to be patient with yourself as you start connecting with others again. Give yourself grace to navigate the new beginnings and celebrate the memories you are making.

Affirm

Scripture Memorization: Write the following scripture and post it somewhere you'll see it every day, maybe it's a bathroom mirror, refrigerator, or your home office. Memorize it and refer to it when you feel alone at the bottom of the ocean.

"Do nothing out of selfish ambition or vain conceit. Rather, in humility value others above yourselves, not looking to your own interests but each of you to the interests of the others." —Philippians 2:3–4

Notate

Scripture Application: Reading the verse in Philippians 2:3–4, how can this verse be applied to your life today?

_____
_____
_____
_____
_____
_____
_____
_____
_____
_____

Craft

Creative Exercise: Be courageous, create a list of small challenges you can undertake to build your courage to rejoin your community.

_____

_____

_____

_____

_____

_____

_____

_____

_____

_____

_____

_____

_____

_____

_____

_____

_____

Honor

Prayer: *Heavenly Father, I ask for forgiveness for my shortcomings in my friendships. I pray, Lord for strength and courage to step out again as I work on rebuilding connections. I pray that you bring to me those who you want to be in my life for many years to come. I pray, Father, that this time around, I can make these connections stick and last for the rest of my life. Thank you, Lord, for the beautiful souls you'll undoubtedly send my way, Amen.*

Observe

- **Exercise Option 1:** Social media: If you are on social media, I want to encourage you to share a snippet of your personal life and why community is important to you. If you have been absent in the lives of others, this is a good opportunity to also share that you are stepping outside more and ready to get back to spending time with others. You could even go as far as asking if anyone would be up for getting together at a local coffee shop or restaurant (group or individual, up to you).

- **Exercise Option 2:** Not on social media: If you aren't on social media, I want to encourage you to reach out to 1–3 people and share a snippet of your personal life and why spending time with them is important to you. If you have been absent in their lives up to this point, this is a good time for you to address this and invite them to meet up with you at a local coffee shop or restaurant. (You can meet individually 1:1 or as a group, the choice is yours.)

- **Journal:** Reflecting on how you felt during the last exercise, answer the following questions.

After putting myself back out there again, I felt:

_____

_____

_____

_____

_____

_____

_____

Rebuilding my community means _____ to me.

_____

_____

_____

_____

_____

_____

Rebuild

What fears do you have about putting yourself back out there and connecting with others again?

_____

_____

_____

_____

_____

_____

_____

_____

_____

_____

_____

_____

What will help you overcome those fears?

_____

_____

_____

_____

_____

_____

_____

_____

_____

_____

_____

_____

_____

_____

Emerge

Action Taking Exercise Option 1: Schedule a get-together with 1–3 people, set the date, time, and place. You should have this done within 1–2 weeks of doing this lesson, if possible. Using blank notecards, write each of your guests a handwritten letter letting them know how much they mean to you and how grateful you are they are in your life. You will deliver these in person at your gathering. If the means allow for it, I would also stop and pick up a flower for them, usually a single rose wrapped individually, or (if the budget allowed) I would pick up a small bundle of daisies. Write down your plans for your gathering.

Date of Gathering   Location of Gathering

Guest Name   Sentiment to Give

1.

2.

3.

Action Taking Exercise Option 2: In a season of isolation? That is ok. I've been there too! This is the time for you to begin thinking about where you might be able to find community. A church. The gym. A neighbor. Just start taking steps in this direction and understand that this takes time—and that's ok.

Community Ideas

Dedicate

How can prayer help you form deeper connections and fellowship with others?

_____

_____

_____

_____

_____

_____

The person I am choosing to be for my friends is...

_____

_____

_____

_____

_____

_____

_____

_____

Declaration Statements

"I am" statement: Write a statement about who you feel you are in this very moment. _Example: I am an authentic friend.._

I am

_____

_____

"I hope to be" statement: Write a statement about who you hope to be by the end of this book. _Example: I hope to be an encouragement to those who need me to be._

I hope to be

_____

_____

Chapter Fifteen
Rediscovery of Joy

Rediscovering joy is something that many people think isn't achievable. I was transformed, by simply making the decision to paint the walls months after choosing paint chips. All of this was only possible by following all the steps that led to this point and heeding God's nudge to get up off the couch and move. God is tenderly calling to you now. He is asking you to take a big step forward towards rediscovering your joy. Will you heed His call?

Affirm

Scripture Memorization: Write the following scripture and post it somewhere you'll see it every day. Maybe it's a bathroom mirror, refrigerator, or your home office. Memorize it and refer to it when you feel alone at the bottom of the ocean.

"Consider it pure joy, my brothers and sisters, whenever you face trials of many kinds." —James 1:2

Notate

Scripture Application: Reading the verse in James 1:2, how can this verse be applied to your life today?

_____

_____

_____

_____

_____

_____

_____

_____

_____

_____

_____

Craft

Creative Exercise: In the center of this page is the word "happiness". Using the lines coming from the circle, add short descriptions of actions you need to take to reach happiness. This can be something like painting walls in your house, organizing, exercising, praying more, etc. Write down everything you think of.

Honor

Prayer: *Heavenly Father, I am so grateful for all you have done to help me get out of the bottom of the ocean and back on solid ground. I am so thankful for the lessons you've shown me along the way and the purpose you've given me in all of my pain. Thank you for reminding me that joy is present within me even during my most difficult times, that it never leaves me and is always there waiting for me to discover it again. Thank you, Lord, for opening up my heart and allowing me the chance to feel pure joy again, Amen.*

Observe

- **Exercise:** Look back through all the exercises you have completed up until this point. Study each of the moments in time that captured your journey. Make a mental note of how you feel looking back to where you are today.
- **Journal:** A look back at how far you've come.

Looking back from the beginning of this book until now, my journey in self rediscovery looks like:

_____

_____

_____

_____

_____

_____

_____

_____

_____

_____

I feel _____ about my journey through this book.

_____

_____

_____

_____

_____

_____

_____

_____

_____

_____

Rebuild

Looking at your mind map, what is one thing you can begin today to reach your goal of happiness? Write about why this is important to you to do.

_____

_____

_____

_____

_____

_____

_____

_____

_____

_____

_____

_____

Today I experienced joy in…

_____

_____

_____

_____

_____

_____

_____

_____

_____

_____

_____

Emerge

Action Taking Exercise: It's time to get up and act. The one thing you wrote about that you can begin today to reach your goal of happiness is taking the first step of action to get the ball rolling. (For me it was to purchase the paint, followed by putting paint on the walls, and continuing it until the project was completed.) Use the blank space below to draw or doodle your plan of action.

Dedicate

How I feel after getting started:

_____

_____

_____

Happiness feels like it's (within reach, or still really far away):

_____

_____

_____

How I know I'm on the right path to happiness is:

_____

_____

_____

_____

Declaration Statements

"I am" statement: Write a statement about who you feel you are in this very moment. *Example: I am filled with joy.*

I am

_____

_____

"I hope to be" statement: Write a statement about who you hope to be by the end of this book. *Example: I hope to be joyful in all I do.*

I hope to be

_____

_____

Chapter Sixteen
You Are Authentically Created

You did it! You've reached the end of the book and now it is time to rebrand yourself; embrace your unique identity and purpose. Don't be afraid to share your hardships and how God helped you overcome them. It is through your testimony that others can have hope!

Affirm

Scripture Memorization: Write the following scripture and post it somewhere you'll see it every day. Maybe it's a bathroom mirror, refrigerator, or your home office. Memorize it and refer to it when you feel alone at the bottom of the ocean.

"But in your hearts revere Christ as Lord. Always be prepared to give an answer to everyone who asks. You to give the reason for the hope that you have. But do this with gentleness and respect." —1 Peter 3:15

Notate

Scripture Application: Reading the verse in 1 Peter 3:15, how can this verse be applied to your life today?

_____

_____

_____

_____

_____

_____

_____

_____

_____

_____

_____

_____

Craft

Creative Exercise Mood Board: You can either do this exercise as an art project with magazine cutouts or you can go digital with Pinterest, it is your choice. Pick photos and quotes that align with who you feel you are to your core. Things that light you up, bring you joy, etc. The goal of this is to see you on that board. Use the blank space below to glue items from your moodboard.

Honor

Prayer: *Heavenly Father, we have gone on a journey together from the depths of despair to joy-filled living. Lord, I am excited to be able to start living my life more authentically in a way that is pleasing to you. I pray for strength and guidance as I find my footing during my rebrand. Thank you, Lord, for revealing who I am in you, Amen.*

Observe

- **Mirror Exercise:** Full-length mirror if possible: Look at yourself in the mirror—the whole you. Observe all physical attributes you have. Lock eyes with yourself and smile. This is you, authentically created by God to be you, no one else, beautiful you. You have experienced life's joys and challenges, you've had growth and transformation. You are strong, courageous, beautiful, and loved. Speak out loud, "I accept and love myself as I am, authentically created by God."
- **Journal:** Think back to how you felt during the mirror exercise as you answer these questions.

What emotions came up during the mirror exercise?

_____

_____

_____

_____

_____

_____

_____

_____

_____

_____

_____

_____

How do you feel about the person you saw in the mirror?

_____

_____

_____

_____

_____

_____

What aspects of your authentic self do you appreciate the most?

_____

_____

_____

_____

_____

_____

Rebuild

Looking at my completed mood board, I can clearly see who I am. The things that stick out to me most are:

_____

_____

_____

_____

_____

_____

_____

_____

_____

The one thing I've discovered about myself by participating in this workbook fully is:

_____

_____

_____

_____

_____

_____

_____

_____

_____

_____

_____

_____

Something I am looking forward to in my future is:

_____

_____

_____

_____

_____

_____

_____

_____

_____

_____

_____

_____

_____

Emerge

Action Taking Exercise: It's time to emerge, life is worth living, and I want to encourage you to fully accept your authentic self, be boldly you, and go in confidence. Reach out to your friends and share with them that you finished the book and are ready to share with others your authentic self. If you feel up to hosting a party, I recommend a small gathering in your home with your closest friends who have been with you since Chapter 5.

Date of Gathering   Location of Gathering

Guest Name   To-Do

1.   ☐ _____

2.   ☐ _____

3.   ☐ _____

4.   ☐ _____

5.   ☐ _____

6.   ☐ _____

7.   ☐ _____

8.   ☐ _____

9.   ☐ _____

10.   ☐ _____

11.   ☐ _____

12.

Notes:

Dedicate

What steps can you take to express your authentic self fully in your daily life?

_____

_____

_____

_____

_____

_____

Who I am at my most authentic is…

_____

_____

_____

_____

_____

_____

Declaration Statements

"I am" statement: Write a statement about who you feel you are in this very moment. *Example: I am my most authentic self.*

I am

_____

_____

"I hope to be" statement: Write a statement about who you hope to be by the end of this book. *Example: I hope to be a beacon of light to others so that they can find their way out of the bottom of the ocean..*

I hope to be

_____

_____

A Letter From Shonda

Friend, you did it! When we first started this journey together, you needed a lifeline to help you come up for air. I pray that our time together has helped you learn more about yourself, your friends, and your relationship with God. I know that often when we finish a book, the overwhelming feeling of 'what's next' hits hard. Truth is, you already have the answer to that question: you continue building a life you love.

On days when the weight of your labels threatens to pull you back under, reach for your completed workbook and go back to the beginning to remind yourself of how much you accomplished. Join in on our Facebook Group to connect with others who, like you, have also gone through the exercises in this book and can offer a different perspective.

May you always know that you are never at the bottom of the ocean alone. Jesus is always right there, extending his hand towards you to help pull you to shore.

It's time for you to step into the fullness of your purpose and break free from the chains of expectation. It's time to rediscover yourself, love who you are, and live a life that's Authentically Anchored in Christ.

I'm rooting for you always!
With Grace,
Shonda Ramsey

www.ingramcontent.com/pod-product-compliance
Lightning Source LLC
Chambersburg PA
CBHW041141120626
46547CB00020B/3066